Dare to Bake!

Ady Abreu

CUPCAKE RECIPES TO AWAKEN YOUR
SWEET TOOTH

4880 Lower Valley Road · Atglen, PA 19310

Other Schiffer Books on Related Subjects:

Sugar Art by Geraldine Kidwell and Barbara Green.
ISBN 978-0-7643-3382-8

Cakes for All Occasions by Geraldine Kidwell.
ISBN 978-0-7643-2904-3

The Art of the Wedding Cake by Mary Anne Pirro.
ISBN 978-0-7643-3924-0

Food photography and food styling
by Tania Colamarino

Library of Congress Control Number: 2014956003

Designed by Brenda McCallum
Cover design by Justin Watkinson
Type set in Mr Keningbeck/Anro Pro

ISBN: 978-0-7643-4796-2

Printed in China

Published by Schiffer Publishing, Ltd.
4880 Lower Valley Road
Atglen, PA 19310
Phone: (610) 593-1777
Fax: (610) 593-2002
E-mail: Info@schifferbooks.com

For our complete selection of fine books on this and related subjects, please visit our website at www.schifferbooks.com. You may also write for a free catalog.

This book may be purchased from the publisher. Please try your bookstore first.

We are always looking for people to write books on new and related subjects. If you have an idea for a book, please contact us at proposals@schifferbooks.com.

Schiffer Publishing's titles are available at special discounts for bulk purchases for sales promotions or premiums. Special editions, including personalized covers, corporate imprints, and excerpts can be created in large quantities for special needs. For more information, contact the publisher.

Dedication

To my mother, Iluminada, for understanding that being a baker makes me happier than being an engineer.
To my sister Joaltcris, my brother José Luis, and my dad Isidoro.
To my friends: Tania Colamarino, Lyndon Lapasaran, Raquel Arias, Ana Maria Dominguez
and Huascar Aquino for listening to my ramblings, tolerating my marathonic phone calls and infinite
text messages and for being there for me through thick and thin.
To my amazing customers and Berks County for supporting my business.
And to Sam Miriello: *"You are the butter to my bread, and the breath to my life"*—JC

A party without cake is just a meeting.
Julia Child

Contents

Acknowledgments

Thank you to Peter Schiffer and the amazing team at Schiffer Publishing
for making my dream a reality, and to my editor, Jesse Marth, for his patience and dedication.

Be a Daring Baker!

I have been cooking since a very young age; both my parents worked full time jobs and my siblings and I had to take the responsibility to feed ourselves. Nonetheless, there was never a frozen, pre-packaged, fast food item in sight. Everything we needed to eat we had to cook from scratch, and what was available were always fresh ingredients. Coming from a humble background has taught me to be not only creative, but resourceful.

Many people are intimidated by baking, mostly because it requires a certain level of structure, but it doesn't mean you can't be creative and adventurous, and it certainly doesn't mean you need to be constrained by particular rules.

When people ask me if I have an educational background in baking they are shocked to know that I don't...at all! Not even close...my background is in industrial engineering.

Years before opening my tiny little bake shop in West Reading, Pennsylvania, I had a nice corporate job, but I was getting burned out. I wanted a medium to explore my creativity, so I started playing with cake recipes and working on the artistry of cake decorating in my home kitchen. I felt a great sense of peace and I was mesmerized by how much you can do with a few ingredients found in the pantry. I couldn't stop baking and creating, my fridge was always packed with cakes and cupcakes, and anyone who visited had to take some of my wacky creations with them.

I started my business in 2007 as a part-time project. I rented a lovely shop on my town's main street. It only took a few months for me to realize it would not be possible to be "halfway" in my business, so I decided to take my life savings and go all in.

After five years of running my business as a one-woman show, I realized I had to do something bigger; I needed to separate myself from the pack of cake and cupcake shops that were suddenly popping up all over town.

I was a huge fan of the popular show *Cupcakes Wars* on Food Network, so when one of the producers called me I was in shock. He wanted to know if I was interested in being on the show. I immediately said "Yes!" We talked for a few minutes, I answered some questions, and he told me he would email me an audition form and some instructions. The minute I hung up the phone I thought to myself, "What have I gotten myself into?!"

I competed against three other successful bakers, but I knew my way to the judges' hearts (or stomachs) was to create a unique cupcake on each and every round. Being safe was not an option and the risk paid off! I won!!! Yay!!!

To say the *Cupcake Wars* experience is walk in the park...is a lie! Regardless of whether you are a professional baker or not the competition is mentally, physically, and emotional exhausting... but of course I would do it all over again if I had to.

Right after my *Cupcake Wars* episode aired, customers lined outside of my little shop to buy my cupcakes. It was insane! We baked thousands and thousands of cupcakes. People were so excited to meet me and ask about the show, the judges and the madness! But one question was always a constant: "How do you come up with these creative ideas?" Well, the answer is simple: through curiosity.

To you, holding my book in your hands: As with anything in life, be adventurous, be daring!

My 10 "Baking Commandments"

There are a few simple rules or "commandments" that I follow and that I suggest any first-time baker keep in mind before turning on the oven.

1. Be curious. Don't say you don't like it until you try it. There are probably foods and ingredients in this book that you haven't tasted, seen or heard of before, but don't judge them until you give them a try. If you wish to incorporate a certain level of novelty and creativity into your baking, you have to be open-minded and accept these ingredients for what they are, not judge them by what you thought they'd taste like or by what you expected them to be. Learn to appreciate these new flavors, new textures, and hey!—you might even like them! (Gasp!)

2. Find a great base recipe. Once you find a recipe that you like, you can easily start switching around ingredients and incorporating new ones as you become more comfortable with the recipe. You are not going to know how much you like a recipe until you try it. Research ingredients and flavor combinations that appeal to you, but be open-minded. (See Commandment 1!)

3. Get the right ingredients. Once you find a recipe, make sure you have all its ingredients on hand. It's not much fun to discover that you don't have any baking powder when you have already started mixing!

4. Get the right tools. A good electric mixer and an oven thermometer are vital to successful baking, and also make sure you have the correct pan sizes and tools before you start baking.

5. Test your oven! Make sure your oven is appropriately calibrated before you start baking. Baked dishes can be easily ruined if the oven is too low or too high.

6. Follow instructions. Remember, baking is science—you must respect its nature.

7. Let it be. You simply can't rush the baking process, and cranking up the oven temperature to rush a batch of cupcakes will most likely result in dry and overbaked products.

8. Icing a warm cake or cupcake is never a good idea.

9. It's all about the presentation. No matter how great a dish is, if the display is sloppy, your guests will not be as tempted to try it. After you spend time in the kitchen preparing a dish, make sure it is presented with dignity.

10. Enjoy! Take the time to savor your creations. Have you ever baked something amazing and been so busy with your guests that you don't even take a moment to eat it?! Don't do that to yourself.

The Basic Technique

My main baking technique is pretty basic and easy to follow. Most of my recipes call for a combination of granulated sugar and unsalted butter at the beginning of the process; it's really important to properly cream the butter and the sugar to create air bubbles that will result in a light and fluffy cupcake.

I always use unsalted butter for baking because salted butter tends to be too salty. The butter has to be at room temperature (but if it's at refrigerated temperature, you can always microwave it for a few seconds until it becomes soft). The creaming process normally takes about 7 to 8 minutes on an electric mixer at medium-high speed. You will notice that once the butter and sugar are properly creamed, the mixture becomes very pale in color and fluffy in texture.

Once the butter and the sugar are creamed, the next step is adding the eggs. The eggs have to be at room temperature as well, and should be added one at a time, each one being incorporated into the batter before the next egg is added. This process takes about 2 more minutes.

The flour and the dry ingredients should be mixed as long as necessary to fully incorporate them with the rest of the ingredients. You want to mix until the dry ingredients have soaked up the liquids and the batter is smooth, and only until then, as over-mixing the batter can result in heavy and too-dense cake.

I highly recommend that all the liquids and dairy products you're using be at room temperature, to ensure they will be fully incorporated.

When it comes to flavoring, nothing compares to good quality extracts: pure vanilla extract, pure almond extract, pure lemon extract, and so on. I love oil-based extracts because their flavor and aroma is much more potent than liquid-based extracts. Extracts should be used to enhance and complement the ingredients, not as a main source of flavor.

Cupcakes are delicate creatures and they can be overbaked very easily, so I normally bake them at a lower temperature and for a longer time: at 325° F in a gas oven for 20 to 22 minutes.

Each batter behaves differently—some cupcakes are completely done at 20 minutes and some need a longer cooking time. Test the cupcakes by inserting a toothpick: if it comes out clean the cupcakes are done.

After the cupcakes are baked, allow them to cool down for a few minutes before removing them from the pan. If you try to remove them while they're still hot you might break them! Lastly, you can place them on a cooling rack to allow them to cool down completely.

Baking Essentials

Being a successful baker requires a high level of organization. Before trying any recipe, make sure you have the corresponding ingredients and the following tools and utensils on hand; if you don't, you take the risk of not achieving the expected results.

Basic Tools

- Electric mixer (A stand mixer with the paddle attachment is ideal, but if you have a handheld electric mixer you can certainly make do.)
- Oven thermometer
- Silicone spatula
- Measuring cups
- Measuring spoons
- Mixing bowls
- Sifter
- Ice cream scooper (I use it to scoop the batter into the pans. It helps you keep all your cupcakes one consistent size.)
- Apple corer
- Greaseproof cupcake liners
- Bags and large metal piping tips
- Cupcake pans (with 3.5-fluid-ounce wells)

PART 1

Daring Creations

Whether you are an avid baker or you are just diving into it, I will assure you: the more you bake the more you want to create! In your baking adventures you can easily transition from your basic vanilla or chocolate cupcake into more daring creations by simply adding a few spices, and substituting or adding new ingredients.

Pistachio and Cardamom Cupcakes

This recipe is my one of my all-time favorites. It is my *Cupcake Wars* round one cupcake and it was so well received by the judges that I couldn't not include it in this book. It has every element you could imagine. With the mix of pistachios and cardamom the cupcake is sweet, spicy and crunchy. The dates-and-honey filling is sticky and gooey, and the orange icing adds a touch of freshness. The toasted pistachios and black pepper garnish makes this cupcake a clear home run.

14

Cupcakes

3 cups all-purpose flour
1 tablespoon baking powder
1 teaspoon ground cardamom
½ cup chopped salted pistachios
1 cup buttermilk
½ cup sour cream
¼ cup vegetable oil
1 tablespoon vanilla extract
1 teaspoon almond extract
8 ounces unsalted butter (2 sticks)
2 cups sugar
5 large eggs

Dates and Honey Filling

2 cups pitted dates, chopped
1½ cups water
½ cup honey
1 teaspoon ground cardamom

Toasted Pistachios

½ cup chopped shelled pistachios
½ teaspoon sea salt
½ teaspoon ground black pepper

Orange Cream Cheese Icing

8 ounces unsalted butter (2 sticks)
8 ounces cream cheese
2 tablespoons fresh orange juice
2 tablespoons orange extract
1 tablespoon vanilla extract
½ teaspoon orange food coloring (optional)
Zest of one orange
¼ teaspoon salt
1 lb powdered sugar

Cupcakes

Preheat oven to 325° F. Line a cupcake pan with 24 cupcake liners. Sift the flour and baking powder into a bowl, add cardamom and chopped pistachios and set aside. Combine the buttermilk, sour cream, oil, vanilla extract and almond extract in another bowl and set aside.

In the bowl of an electric mixer fitted with the paddle attachment, cream the butter and sugar until the mixture is lighter in color and fluffy, about 7 minutes on medium-high speed. Lower the speed to medium and add the eggs, one egg at a time, scraping down the sides of the bowl after each addition until fully incorporated, about 2 minutes. Turn the mixer to a lower speed, then add the flour mixture and the buttermilk mixture, alternating between the two, beginning and ending with the flour.

Fill the 24 cupcake liners two-thirds full with batter and bake for 20 to 22 minutes, until the cupcakes are golden and baked through. Cool cupcakes completely.

Filling

Place the chopped dates in a food processor and add the water as it blends, until you get a thick paste.

In a heavy-bottomed saucepan, combine dates, honey and cardamom and cook over medium-low heat until the mixture becomes thicker (15–18 minutes), stirring frequently. Remove from heat and transfer the mixture into a bowl. Cool completely.

Garnish

Spread chopped pistachios evenly on a baking sheet and bake for about 8 minutes at 325° F until golden brown. Remove from heat and season with sea salt and freshly ground black pepper.

Icing

Whip the butter in the bowl of an electric mixer fitted with the paddle attachment at medium-high speed until it is light and fluffy, about 7 minutes. Lower the speed and add the cream cheese, orange juice, orange extract, vanilla, orange food coloring (optional), orange zest and the salt and beat until fully incorporated. Stop the mixer and scrape the sides, then add the powdered sugar and beat for 3 more minutes. Stop the mixer and scrape the sides, then mix for 5 more minutes at medium-high speed. Put the icing into a pastry bag fitted with a large metal tip.

To assemble: Allow the cupcakes to fully cool. Using an apple corer, remove a piece of each cupcake from the center, fill the cupcakes with the date filling, and pipe on the orange icing. Garnish with the toasted pistachios. Enjoy!

24 cupcakes

Hibiscus Flower Cupcakes

Hibiscus flowers grow everywhere in my home country, the Dominican Republic, but they're not normally used in cooking. It wasn't until I started venturing into Mexican cuisine that I discovered this fascinating ingredient. You can find dried hibiscus flowers in the Mexican food section of your grocery store.

The hibiscus flower, when soaked in water, produces a red colored juice, and when that's used in cupcakes it creates a beautiful deep purple batter. Its flavor can be described as sour and citrusy.

I pair this cupcake with a tart passion fruit filling to add an extra punch of tropical flair.

16

Cupcakes

3 cups all-purpose flour
1 tablespoon baking powder
½ teaspoon salt
1 cup hibiscus flower mixture (*See note*)
¼ cup vegetable oil
1 tablespoon vanilla extract
½ teaspoon almond extract
8 ounces unsalted butter (2 sticks)
2 cups sugar
5 large eggs

Passion Fruit Curd Filling

½ cup fresh passion fruit juice
   (about 6 passion fruits)
8 egg yolks
1 cup sugar
1 tablespoon fresh lemon juice
¼ teaspoon salt
4 ounces unsalted butter (1 stick)

Hibiscus Flower Icing

1 lb unsalted butter
¼ cup hibiscus flower mixture (*See note*)
1 tablespoon vanilla extract
¼ teaspoon salt
1 lb powdered sugar

Note: To make the amount of hibiscus flower mixture needed for the Cupcakes and Icing: The day before baking, place 1 cup of dry hibiscus flowers and 1½ cups of water in a container, and soak overnight; on baking day place mixture in the food processor and pulse until the flowers are finely chopped and you get a soft puree.

Cupcakes

Preheat oven to 325° F. Line a cupcake pan with 24 cupcake liners. Sift the flour, baking powder and salt into a bowl and set aside. Combine 1 cup of the hibiscus flower mixture (reserve the remainder for the icing; recipe follows), oil, and vanilla and almond extracts in another bowl and set aside.

In the bowl of an electric mixer fitted with the paddle attachment, cream the butter and sugar until the mixture is light in color and fluffy, about 7 minutes on medium-high speed. Lower the speed to medium and add the eggs, one egg at a time, scraping down the sides of the bowl after each addition until fully incorporated, about 2 minutes. Turn the mixer to a lower speed, then add the flour mixture and the liquids, alternating between the two, beginning and ending with the flour.

Fill the 24 cupcake liners two-thirds full with batter and bake for 20 to 22 minutes, until the cupcakes are golden and baked through. Cool cupcakes completely.

Filling

Cut open passion fruits and scoop out the flesh into a food processor. Pulse until the seeds break, then strain into a bowl to get rid of seeds. Add egg yolks, sugar, lemon juice and salt and beat until all ingredients are mixed well.

In heavy-bottomed, non-stick saucepan melt butter over medium-low heat. Add passion fruit mixture and stir constantly until the mixture starts to thicken; continue to stir constantly for about 10 more minutes until it thickens more. Remove from heat and immediately place in a glass container to set and cool. Cover with plastic wrap, pressing directly onto the surface of the curd to prevent skin from forming. Refrigerate at least 1 hour before using.

Icing

Whip the butter in the bowl of an electric mixer fitted with the paddle attachment on medium-high speed until the butter is light and fluffy, about 7 minutes. Lower the speed and add hibiscus juice mixture, vanilla extract and salt and beat until fully incorporated. Stop the mixer and scrape the sides, then add the powdered sugar and beat for 3 more minutes. Stop the mixer and scrape the sides, then mix for 5 more minutes at medium-high speed. Put the icing into a pastry bag fitted with a large metal tip.

To assemble: Allow the cupcakes to fully cool. Using an apple corer, remove a piece of each cupcake from the center, fill with the passion fruit curd filling, and pipe on the hibiscus flower icing.

24 cupcakes

Tamarind Cupcakes

Oh, tamarind! I love-love tamarinds! This delicious fruit is a bit odd looking; it is a pod with a sweet and very sour but creamy pulp and big brown seeds. My grandmother used to have a gigantic tamarind tree in her backyard, so big that the branches would go over her kitchen roof. During our summer vacations we would visit her and all the grandchildren would climb on top of the kitchen roof and reach out to the tamarind beans, and eat them until our mouths were sore.
The good old days! You can find tamarind paste as well as guava paste, used here in the filling, in the produce sections of Latino or Asian supermarkets.

Cupcakes

3 cups all-purpose flour
1 tablespoon baking powder
½ teaspoon salt
1 cup tamarind juice (*See note*)
¼ cup vegetable oil
1 tablespoon vanilla extract
½ teaspoon almond extract
8 ounces unsalted butter (2 sticks)
2 cups sugar
5 large eggs

Guava Filling

2 cups guava paste
½ cup water
1 tablespoon lemon juice
½ cup sugar

Guava Icing

1 lb unsalted butter
½ cup guava paste
1 tablespoon vanilla extract
½ teaspoon almond extract
¼ teaspoon salt
1 lb powdered sugar

Note: To make the tamarind juice, the day before baking place 1 cup of tamarind paste and 1½ cups of water in a container, and soak overnight; on baking day place mixture in the food processor and pulse until the tamarind pulp and the seeds separate. Strain the juice into a bowl, and discard the flesh and loose seeds.

Cupcakes

Preheat oven to 325° F. Line a cupcake pan with 24 cupcake liners. Sift the flour, baking powder and salt into a bowl and set aside. Combine 1 cup of the tamarind juice, oil, and vanilla and almond extracts in another bowl and set aside.

In the bowl of an electric mixer fitted with the paddle attachment, cream the butter and sugar until the mixture is lighter in color and fluffy, about 7 minutes on medium-high speed. Lower the speed to medium and add the eggs, one egg at a time, scraping down the sides of the bowl after each addition until fully incorporated, about 2 minutes. Turn the mixer to a lower speed, then add the flour mixture and the liquids, alternating between the two, beginning and ending with the flour.

Fill the 24 cupcake liners two-thirds full with batter and bake for 20 to 22 minutes, until the cupcakes are golden and baked through. Cool cupcakes completely.

Filling

Combine all ingredients in a heavy-bottomed saucepan. Whisk together and cook at medium heat, stirring constantly until mixture thickens, 8 to 10 minutes.

Remove from heat and place in a glass bowl. Let cool to room temperature.

Icing

Whip the butter in the bowl of an electric mixer fitted with the paddle attachment on medium-high speed until light and fluffy, about 7 minutes; lower the speed and add the guava paste, vanilla, almond extract and salt and beat until fully incorporated. Stop the mixer and scrape the sides, then add the powdered sugar and beat for 3 more minutes. Stop the mixer and scrape the sides, then mix for 5 more minutes at medium-high speed. Put the icing into a pastry bag fitted with a large metal tip.

To assemble: Allow the cupcakes to fully cool. Using an apple corer, remove a piece of each cupcake from the center, fill the cupcakes with the guava filling, and pipe on the guava icing.

24 cupcakes

Pomegranate Ginger Cupcakes

Spices are definitely my thing. I own every spice that I have put my hands on or tasted! If used well, spices can add a fantastic extra touch to any baked creation.

I made this cupcake during round two of *Cupcake Wars,* and judge Candace Nelson (owner of Sprinkles Cupcakes, and Queen Bee of the cupcake world) truly appreciated the way I captured the richness and exotic flavors of the spices—ginger, cinnamon and nutmeg. This is a cupcake that can add an interesting twist to your typical holiday baking.

Cupcakes

3 cups all-purpose flour
1 tablespoon baking powder
½ teaspoon salt
½ teaspoon ground cinnamon
½ teaspoon ground nutmeg
¼ cup fresh ginger, grated
¾ cup pomegranate juice
¼ cup vegetable oil
1 tablespoon vanilla extract
½ teaspoon almond extract
8 ounces unsalted butter (2 sticks)
2 cups sugar
5 large eggs

Apricot Filling

2 cups dried apricots, chopped
1½ cups water
½ cup sugar
½ teaspoon ground cinnamon

Ginger Icing

1 lb unsalted butter
2 tablespoons heavy whipping cream
2 tablespoons fresh ginger, grated
1 tablespoon vanilla extract
1 teaspoon almond extract
¼ teaspoon salt
1 lb powdered sugar

Cupcakes

Preheat oven to 325° F. Line a cupcake pan with 24 cupcake liners. Sift the flour, baking powder, salt, cinnamon and nutmeg into a bowl, add ginger and set aside. Combine the pomegranate juice, oil, and vanilla and almond extracts in another bowl and set aside.

In the bowl of an electric mixer fitted with the paddle attachment, cream the butter and sugar until the mixture is lighter in color and fluffy, about 7 minutes on medium-high speed. Lower the speed to medium and add the eggs, one egg at a time, scraping down the sides of the bowl after each addition until fully incorporated, about 2 minutes. Turn the mixer to a lower speed, then add the flour mixture and the liquids, alternating between the two, beginning and ending with the flour.

Fill the 24 cupcake liners two-thirds full with batter and bake for 20 to 22 minutes, until the cupcakes are golden and baked through. Cool cupcakes completely.

Filling

Place chopped apricots in a food processor and add the water as it blends, until you get a thick paste. In a heavy-bottomed saucepan combine apricot, sugar and cinnamon and cook over medium-low heat until the mixture becomes thicker, about 15 to 18 minutes. Stir frequently. Transfer the mixture to a dish and cool completely.

Icing

Whip the butter in the bowl of an electric mixer fitted with the paddle attachment at medium-high speed until light and fluffy, about 7 minutes; lower the speed and add the heavy whipping cream, ginger, vanilla extract, almond extract and the salt and beat until fully incorporated. Stop the mixer and scrape the sides, then add the powdered sugar and beat for 3 more minutes. Stop the mixer and scrape the sides, then mix for 5 more minutes at medium-high speed. Put the icing into a pastry bag fitted with a large metal tip.

To assemble: Allow the cupcakes to fully cool. Using an apple corer, remove a piece of each cupcake from the center, fill the cupcakes with the apricot filling, and pipe on the ginger icing.

24 cupcakes

Spiced Chocolate Cupcakes

Just by adding cayenne pepper to this decadent and chocolatey cupcake, you can transform this recipe into an extraordinary creation.

The meringue filling is our beloved typical Dominican icing that we call suspiro ("sigh" in English) for its airy and fluffy texture.

Cupcakes

1¾ cup all-purpose flour
¾ cup unsweetened cocoa powder
½ teaspoon cayenne pepper
1½ teaspoon baking powder
1½ teaspoon baking soda
½ teaspoon salt
2 cups buttermilk
½ cup vegetable oil

1 tablespoon vanilla extract
1 teaspoon almond extract
2 cups sugar
2 large eggs

Meringue Filling

3 cups sugar
1 cup of water
6 large egg whites at room temperature

2 tablespoons light corn syrup
1 teaspoon vanilla extract

Cayenne Pepper Ganache

2 cups semisweet chocolate chips
2 cups heavy whipping cream
2 tablespoons unsalted butter
½ teaspoon cayenne pepper

Cupcakes

Preheat oven to 325° F. Line a cupcake pan with 24 cupcake liners. Sift the flour, cocoa powder, cayenne pepper, baking powder, baking soda and salt into a bowl. Combine buttermilk, oil, and vanilla and almond extracts in another bowl and set aside.

In the bowl of an electric mixer fitted with the paddle attachment, mix eggs and sugar, until the eggs are fully incorporated, about 3 minutes on medium speed. Turn the mixer to a lower speed, then add the flour mixture and the liquids, alternating between the two, beginning and ending with the flour.

Fill the 24 cupcake liners two-thirds full with batter and bake for 20 to 22 minutes, until the cupcakes are baked through. Cool cupcakes completely.

Filling

Before using the stand mixer, make sure it is completely clean and clear of greasy residues, because grease will ruin the filling. To do so, wipe the inside of the bowl with a paper kitchen towel dampened in white vinegar.

In a small saucepan combine sugar and water and cook at medium heat, stirring slowly until the sugar dissolves. Let the syrup cook until it begins to boil; it will become clear in color.

While the syrup is cooking, place egg whites in a stand mixer fitted with the whisk attachment and beat at high speed. The egg whites will become frothy; continue to beat until they have a thick and foamy consistency. Make sure the egg whites are beaten well throughout the bowl, continuing to beat until the mixture becomes stiff enough to hold peaks.

Once the syrup is boiling and clear (no grains of sugar in sight!), let it cook for about 2 minutes, making sure it doesn't turn brown. Remove the sugar syrup from the heat. Immediately start beating the egg whites again at high speed, and very slowly start adding the syrup a little at a time, continuing this process until you pour all the syrup. Add the corn syrup and continue to beat for an additional 2 to 3 minutes until the meringue gets thick. Finally, add the vanilla extract. Beat for a few extra minutes until you see stiff peaks and the meringue is thick and smooth.

Ganache

Combine semisweet chocolate chips, heavy cream and butter in a heatproof glass bowl and cook on top of a double boiler, stirring constantly until all the chocolate has melted.

(You can also combine the chips and heavy cream in a microwave-safe glass bowl and microwave in increments of 30 seconds, stirring in between, until the chocolate is completely melted. Then stir in the butter until completely melted.)

Stir in cayenne pepper.

To assemble: Allow the cupcakes to fully cool. Using an apple corer, remove a piece of each cupcake from the center, fill the cupcakes with the meringue filling and finally, dip each cupcake individually in the lukewarm ganache.

24 cupcakes

Pear and Cranberry Cupcakes

I always think of pears as the wholesome, quieter, less sassy sister of the apples. However, don't let the subtlety of this fruit discourage you from elevating it to a whole new level. Here, the sour cranberries mixed into the batter, together with the goat cheese in the icing, adds the right amount of tang. My favorite pears for baking are Bartlett pears.

Cupcakes

3 cups all-purpose flour
1 tablespoon baking powder
½ teaspoon salt
½ cup dried cranberries
1 cup diced pears (about 1½ pears)
½ cup buttermilk
¼ cup vegetable oil
1 tablespoon vanilla extract
½ teaspoon almond extract
8 ounces unsalted butter (2 sticks)
2 cups sugar
5 large eggs

Goat Cheese and Honey Icing

8 ounces unsalted butter (2 sticks)
8 ounces goat cheese
¼ cup honey
1 tablespoon vanilla extract
½ teaspoon almond extract
¼ teaspoon salt
1 lb powdered sugar

Toasted Almonds for Garnish

1 cup sliced almonds

Cupcakes

Preheat oven to 325° F. Line a cupcake pan with 24 cupcake liners. Sift the flour, baking powder and salt into a bowl, add cranberries and set aside. Peel and core the pears and dice into half-inch cubes. Combine buttermilk, oil, and vanilla and almond extracts in another bowl and set aside.

In the bowl of an electric mixer fitted with the paddle attachment, cream the butter and sugar until the mixture is lighter in color and fluffy, about 7 minutes on medium-high speed. Lower the speed to medium and add the eggs, one egg at a time, scraping down the sides of the bowl after each addition until fully incorporated, about 2 minutes. Turn the mixer to a lower speed, then add the flour mixture and the liquids, alternating between the two, beginning and ending with the flour. Fold in the diced pears by hand.

Fill the 24 cupcake liners two-thirds full with batter and bake for 20 to 22 minutes, until the cupcakes are golden and baked through. Cool cupcakes completely.

Icing

Whip the butter in the bowl of an electric mixer fitted with the paddle attachment at medium-high speed until the butter is light and fluffy, about 7 minutes; lower the speed and add the goat cheese, honey, vanilla and almond extracts and salt and beat until fully incorporated. Stop the mixer and scrape the sides, then add the powdered sugar and beat for 3 more minutes. Stop the mixer and scrape the sides, then mix for 5 more minutes at medium-high speed. Put the icing into a pastry bag fitted with a large metal tip.

Garnish

Spread almonds evenly on a baking sheet and bake until golden brown, about 8 minutes at 325° F.

To assemble: Allow the cupcakes to fully cool. Pipe on the goat cheese icing and sprinkle the toasted almonds on top.

24 cupcakes

Mango and Saffron Cupcakes

Mangoes are tropical fruits that are in season during the month of August. Mango cupcakes are one of the best-sellers in my shop, but here I'm transforming this cupcake into a more adventurous creation by adding saffron.

I was introduced to saffron about 13 years ago and I've been enchanted by this distinctive and versatile spice ever since; saffron is commonly used in savory cuisine, but here, along with the cardamom, it adds an unmistakable exotic twist. This cupcake is paired with an aromatic icing featuring browned butter and cardamom. If you really want to kick it up a notch, try this daring creation and you won't be disappointed.

26

Cupcakes

3 cups all-purpose flour
1 tablespoon baking powder
½ teaspoon salt
1 teaspoon ground saffron
1½ cup diced mangoes (about 2 very
   ripe mangoes)
¼ cup vegetable oil
1 tablespoon vanilla extract
½ teaspoon almond extract
8 ounces unsalted butter (2 sticks)
2 cups sugar
5 large eggs

Browned Butter Cardamom Icing

1 lb unsalted butter
¼ cup heavy whipping cream
½ teaspoon ground cardamom
¼ teaspoon salt
1 tablespoon vanilla extract
1 lb powdered sugar

Cupcakes

Preheat oven to 325° F. Line a cupcake pan with 24 cupcake liners. Sift the flour, baking powder, salt and saffron into a bowl and set aside.

Peel and cube mangoes and discard the pits; you can dice the mango by hand into small pieces or place the mango cubes in the food processor and blend until you get small chunks. Combine diced mango, oil, and vanilla and almond extracts in another bowl and set aside.

In the bowl of an electric mixer fitted with the paddle attachment, cream the butter and sugar until the mixture is lighter in color and fluffy, about 7 minutes on medium-high speed. Lower the speed to medium and add the eggs, one egg at a time, scraping down the sides of the bowl after each addition until fully incorporated, about 2 minutes. Turn the mixer to a lower speed, then add the flour mixture and the liquids, alternating between the two, beginning and ending with the flour.

Fill the 24 cupcake liners two-thirds full with batter and bake for 20 to 22 minutes, until the cupcakes are golden and baked through. Cool cupcakes completely.

Icing

Chop butter into cubes and place in a small saucepan. Cook over medium heat until the sides start browning. Remove from heat and let cool to room temperature. Allow the butter to go back to its solid state; if you wish to speed up the process you can take the butter out of the pan, put it in a glass container and place in the refrigerator for about 20 minutes.

Whip the butter and heavy whipping cream in the bowl of an electric mixer fitted with the paddle attachment on medium-high speed until the mix is fluffy, about 7 minutes; lower the speed and add the cardamom, vanilla and salt, and beat until fully incorporated. Stop the mixer and scrape the sides, then add the powdered sugar and beat for 3 more minutes. Stop the mixer and scrape the sides, then mix for 5 more minutes at medium-high speed. Put the icing into a pastry bag fitted with a metal tip.

To assemble: Allow the cupcakes to fully cool. Pipe on the browned butter cardamom icing.

24 cupcakes

Coconut Curry Cupcakes

Coconut cupcakes are my mom's favorite and I wanted to challenge her by having her try them with an ingredient that is a bit more unconventional. Enter: curry. Coconut and curry in Asian cuisine is the equivalent of peanut butter and jelly...separately they are great, but together they're dynamite! The lime flavor in the filling and the icing adds a sweet and tangy fresh touch.

Cupcakes

3 cups all-purpose flour
1 tablespoon baking powder
1 teaspoon curry powder
½ teaspoon salt
½ cup unsweetened shredded coconut
1 cup buttermilk
¼ cup vegetable oil
1 tablespoon vanilla extract
½ teaspoon almond extract
8 ounces unsalted butter (2 sticks)
2 cups sugar
5 large eggs

Lime Curd Filling

8 egg yolks
½ cup fresh lime juice
1 tablespoon lime extract
1 cup sugar
¼ teaspoon salt
4 ounces unsalted butter (1 stick)

Lime Icing

1 lb unsalted butter
3 tablespoons fresh lime juice
1 tablespoon vanilla extract
1 teaspoon almond extract
1 tablespoon lime extract
¼ teaspoon salt
Zest of 1 lime
1 lb powdered sugar
Green food coloring (optional)

Cupcakes

Preheat oven to 325° F. Line a cupcake pan with 24 cupcake liners. Sift the flour, baking powder, curry powder and salt into a bowl, then add the shredded coconut and set aside. Combine the buttermilk, oil, and vanilla and almond extracts in another bowl and set aside. In the bowl of an electric mixer fitted with the paddle attachment, cream the butter and sugar until the mixture is lighter in color and fluffy, about 7 minutes on medium-high speed. Lower the speed to medium and add the eggs, one egg at a time, scraping down the sides of the bowl after each addition until fully incorporated, about 2 minutes. Turn the mixer to a lower speed, then add the flour mixture and the liquids, alternating between the two, beginning and ending with the flour.

Fill the 24 cupcake liners two-thirds full with batter and bake for 20 to 22 minutes, until the cupcakes are golden and baked through. Cool cupcakes completely.

Filling

Combine the yolks, lime juice, lime extract, sugar and salt in a glass bowl and beat until all ingredients are mixed well. In a heavy-bottomed saucepan melt butter over low heat, add lime mixture, and stir constantly until the mixture starts to thicken. Continue to stir for about 10 more minutes until it thickens more. Remove from heat and immediately place in a glass container to set and cool. Cover with plastic wrap, pressing directly onto the surface of the curd to prevent skin from forming. Refrigerate at least 1 hour before using.

Icing

Whip the butter in the bowl of an electric mixer fitted with the paddle attachment at medium-high speed until the mixture is light and fluffy, about 7 minutes; lower the speed and add the lime juice, vanilla, almond and lime extracts, salt, lime zest and food coloring. Beat until fully incorporated. Stop the mixer and scrape the sides, then add the powdered sugar and beat for 3 more minutes. Stop the mixer and scrape the sides, then mix for 5 more minutes at medium-high speed. Put the icing into a pastry bag fitted with a large metal tip.

To assemble: Allow the cupcakes to fully cool. Using an apple corer, remove a piece of each cupcake from the center, fill the cupcakes with the lime curd filling, and pipe on the lime icing.

24 cupcakes

Chocolate Stout Beer Cupcakes

This was one of the three kinds of cupcakes I prepared during the second round of *Cupcake Wars*. I wanted to include a chocolate cupcake somehow, and I also wanted to keep using the challenge ingredients that were given to the contestants, so that our team's cupcakes were consistent with the theme, which was the celebration of the California Renaissance Faire. I decided to infuse this moist chocolate cupcake with an extra stout beer, and add sweetness and saltiness using the caramel sauce.

Cupcakes

1¾ cup all-purpose flour
¾ cup unsweetened cocoa
1½ teaspoon baking powder
1½ teaspoon baking soda
½ teaspoon salt
2 cups reduced extra stout b...
  (*See note*)
½ cup vegetable oil
1 tablespoon vanilla extract
1 teaspoon almond extract
2 cups sugar
2 large eggs

Salted Caramel Filling

½ cup water
1 cup sugar
½ cup heavy whipping cream
4 tablespoons unsalted butter
½ teaspoon salt

Stout Beer Icing

1 lb unsalted butter
¼ cup reduced beer (*See note*)
1 tablespoon vanilla extract
1 teaspoon almond extract
¼ teaspoon salt
1 lb powdered sugar

Note: To make reduced beer, in a ...
bottomed saucepan cook 4½ cup...
stout beer at medium heat until r...
about half the volume. Remove f...
and cool to room temperature. T...
the total amount you will need fo...
cupcakes and the icing.

... F and line a cupcake pan with 24 cupcake liners. Sift the flour, cocoa
... er, baking soda and salt into a bowl. Combine 2 cups of reduced beer,
... mond extracts in another bowl and set aside.

... ic mixer fitted with the paddle attachment, mix eggs and sugar until
... orated, about 3 minutes on medium speed. Turn the mixer to a lower
... ur mixture and the liquids, alternating between the two, beginning
... ur.

... ners two-thirds full with batter and bake for 20 to 22 minutes, until
... through. Cool cupcakes completely.

... ed, non-stick saucepan combine water and sugar. Stir lightly and
... emperature until the water has evaporated and the sugar starts
... amber color, about 15 minutes. If sugar crystals form on the side
... them off with a dampened pastry brush.

... combine heavy whipping cream, butter and salt and cook at low
... etely melted.

... ture from the heat and slowly pour into the heavy cream mixture,
... whisk, until both mixtures are well incorporated. Set aside and

... of an electric mixer fitted with the paddle attachment at medium-
... is light and fluffy, about 7 minutes. Lower the speed and add the
... uced beer, vanilla and almond extracts and the salt and beat until
... e mixer and scrape the sides, then add the powdered sugar and
... op the mixer and scrape the sides, then mix for 5 more minutes
... the icing into a pastry bag fitted with a large metal tip.

... cakes to fully cool. Using an apple corer, remove a piece of each
... l the cupcakes with the salted caramel filling, and pipe on the
... h salted caramel.

Red Wine and Cherry Cupcakes

Another recipe from *Cupcake Wars*!
The cherries–red wine combination makes this
cupcake cheerful and sophisticated.

32

Cupcakes

3 cups all-purpose flour
1 tablespoon baking powder
½ teaspoon salt
1 cup pitted sour cherries
    (drained, if canned), chopped
½ cup red wine (Merlot recommended)
¼ cup vegetable oil
1 tablespoon vanilla extract
½ teaspoon cherry extract
½ teaspoon almond extract
8 ounces unsalted butter (2 sticks)
2 cups sugar
5 large eggs

Cherry and Almond Filling

1 15-ounce can of pitted sour cherries,
    drained
½ cup red wine (Merlot recommended),
    divided
½ cup heavy whipping cream
½ cup sugar
1 teaspoon cherry extract
1 teaspoon almond extract
2 tablespoons cornstarch

Red Wine and Cherry Icing

1 lb unsalted butter
½ cup Cherry and Almond Filling
    (recipe above)
1 tablespoon vanilla extract
¼ teaspoon salt
1 lb powdered sugar

Cupcakes

Preheat oven to 325° F. Line a cupcake pan with 24 cupcake liners. Sift the flour, baking powder and salt into a bowl, and set aside.

Drain and chop the sour cherries and combine with wine, oil, vanilla, cherry and almond extracts in another bowl and set aside.

In the bowl of an electric mixer fitted with the paddle attachment, cream the butter and sugar until the mixture is lighter in color and fluffy, about 7 minutes on medium-high speed. Lower the speed to medium and add the eggs, one egg at a time, scraping down the sides of the bowl after each addition until fully incorporated, about 2 minutes. Turn the mixer to a lower speed, then add the flour mixture and the liquids, alternating between the two, beginning and ending with the flour.

Fill the 24 cupcake liners two-thirds full with batter and bake for 20 to 22 minutes, until the cupcakes are golden and baked through. Cool cupcakes completely.

Filling

Puree the sour cherries in a food processor and transfer to a saucepan. Reserve 3 tablespoons of the wine and set aside. Add the remaining wine, heavy whipping cream, sugar, cherry and almond extracts and cook at medium temperature for 10 to 12 minutes, stirring frequently to keep the cherries from sticking to the bottom of the pan.

In a separate container dissolve the 2 tablespoons of cornstarch in the 3 reserved tablespoons of wine and whisk together with a fork until all lumps have disappeared. Pour corn starch mixture into the cherry mixture. Stir and cook for an additional minute; the filling will thicken immediately.

Remove the filling from the heat and cool to room temperature. Store in the refrigerator until needed.

Icing

Whip the butter in the bowl of an electric mixer fitted with the paddle attachment at medium-high speed until the butter is light and fluffy, about 7 minutes. Lower the speed and add the ½ cup of Cherry and Almond Filling, vanilla extract and the salt and beat until fully incorporated. Stop the mixer and scrape the sides, then add the powdered sugar and beat for 3 more minutes. Stop the mixer and scrape the sides, then mix for 5 more minutes at medium-high speed. Put the icing into a pastry bag fitted with a large metal tip.

To assemble: Allow the cupcakes to fully cool. Using an apple corer, remove a piece of each cupcake from the center, fill the cupcakes with cherry and almond filling, and pipe on the cherry icing.

Cranberry Orange Cupcakes

If you are looking for a unique Thanksgiving cupcake this is it! Refreshing orange and tart seasonal cranberries are paired with a sinfully delicious cream cheese icing...and it's topped to perfection with fragrant, sweet-and-salty toasted walnuts.

Cupcakes

3 cups all-purpose flour

1 tablespoon baking powder

½ teaspoon salt

1 cup dried cranberries

½ cup orange puree (*See note*)

½ cup buttermilk

¼ cup vegetable oil

1 tablespoon vanilla extract

1 tablespoon orange extract

½ teaspoon almond extract

8 ounces unsalted butter (2 sticks)

2 cups sugar

5 large eggs

Cream Cheese Icing

8 ounces unsalted butter (2 sticks)

8 ounces cream cheese

1 tablespoon vanilla extract

½ teaspoon almond extract

¼ teaspoon salt

1 lb powdered sugar

Toasted Caramelized Walnut Garnish

1 cup chopped walnuts

¼ cup water

½ cup sugar

½ teaspoon salt

Note: To make orange puree, cut 1 medium seedless orange in half and then cut each half in four pieces. Blend in a food processor with ¼ cup of water until you get a soft puree.

Cupcakes

Preheat oven to 325° F. Line a cupcake pan with 24 cupcake liners. Sift the flour, baking powder and salt into a bowl, add cranberries and set aside.

Combine ½ cup of the orange puree, buttermilk, oil, and vanilla, orange and almond extracts in another bowl and set aside.

In the bowl of an electric mixer fitted with the paddle attachment, cream the butter and sugar until the mixture is lighter in color and fluffy, about 7 minutes on medium-high speed. Lower the speed to medium and add the eggs, one egg at a time, scraping down the sides of the bowl after each addition until fully incorporated, about 2 minutes. Turn the mixer to a lower speed, then add the flour mixture and the liquids, alternating between the two, beginning and ending with the flour.

Fill the 24 cupcake liners two-thirds full with batter and bake for 20 to 22 minutes, until the cupcakes are golden and baked through. Cool cupcakes completely.

Icing

Whip the butter in the bowl of an electric mixer fitted with the paddle attachment at medium-high speed until the butter is light and fluffy, about 7 minutes. Lower the speed and add the cream cheese, vanilla and almond extracts and the salt and beat until fully incorporated. Stop the mixer and scrape the sides, then add the powdered sugar and beat for 3 more minutes. Stop the mixer and scrape the sides, then mix for 5 more minutes at medium-high speed. Put the icing into a pastry bag fitted with a large metal tip.

Garnish

Spread walnuts on a baking sheet in a single layer and bake 12 to 15 minutes at 325° F, checking frequently and stirring, making sure they toast evenly.

Meanwhile, combine water and sugar in small heavy-bottomed non-stick saucepan, stir lightly, and cook at medium-high temperature until the water has evaporated and the sugar starts browning and it turns into an amber color, about 15 minutes. If sugar crystals form on the side of the pan you can brush them off with a dampened pastry brush.

Remove walnuts from the oven and coat with the sugar mixture. Cool to room temperature.

To assemble: Allow the cupcakes to fully cool. Using a large metal tip, pipe on the cream cheese icing. Garnish with the toasted walnuts.

24 cupcakes

Pumpkin Stout Beer Cupcake

I created this cupcake for our town's fall Pretzel and Beer Festival. I wanted to incorporate a seasonal element into it, so I thought pumpkin was the perfect ingredient. The bitterness of the beer adds depth to the flavor of the cupcake, and the salted caramel and crunchy pretzels add decadence and texture.

Cupcakes

3 cups all-purpose flour
1 tablespoon baking powder
1 teaspoon ground cinnamon
½ teaspoon ground nutmeg
½ teaspoon salt
½ cup reduced extra stout beer (*See note*)
¾ cup pure canned pumpkin
¼ cup vegetable oil
1 tablespoon vanilla extract
½ teaspoon almond extract
8 ounces unsalted butter (2 sticks)
2 cups sugar
5 large eggs
Salty pretzels for garnish

Salted Caramel Filling

See page 31 for recipe and instructions.

Cinnamon and Beer Icing

1 lb unsalted butter
¼ cup reduced extra stout beer
  (*See note*)
1 tablespoon ground cinnamon
1 tablespoon vanilla extract
1 teaspoon almond extract
¼ teaspoon salt
1 lb powdered sugar

Note: To make reduced beer, in a heavy-bottomed saucepan cook 2 cups of extra stout beer at medium heat until reduced to about half the volume. Remove from heat and cool to room temperature. This makes the total amount you will need for the cupcakes and the icing.

Cupcakes

Preheat oven to 325° F. Line a cupcake pan with 24 cupcake liners. Sift the flour, baking powder, cinnamon, nutmeg and salt into a bowl, set aside.

Combine ½ cup of the reduced beer, pumpkin, oil, and vanilla and almond extracts in another bowl and set aside.

In the bowl of an electric mixer fitted with the paddle attachment, cream the butter and sugar until the mixture is lighter in color and fluffy, about 7 minutes on medium-high speed. Lower the speed to medium and add the eggs, one egg at a time, scraping down the sides of the bowl after each addition until fully incorporated, about 2 minutes. Turn the mixer to a lower speed, then add the flour mixture and the liquids, alternating between the two, beginning and ending with the flour.

Fill the 24 cupcake liners two-thirds full with batter and bake for 20 to 22 minutes, until the cupcakes are golden and baked through. Cool cupcakes completely.

Icing

Whip the butter in the bowl of an electric mixer fitted with the paddle attachment at medium-high speed until the butter is light and fluffy, about 7 minutes. Lower the speed and add the beer, cinnamon, vanilla and almond extracts, and the salt and beat until fully incorporated. Stop the mixer and scrape the sides, then add the powdered sugar and beat for 3 more minutes. Stop the mixer and scrape the sides, then mix for 5 more minutes at medium-high speed. Put the icing into a pastry bag fitted with a large metal tip.

To assemble: Allow the cupcakes to fully cool. Using an apple corer, remove a piece of each cupcake from the center, fill the cupcakes with salted caramel filling, and pipe on the beer icing. Drizzle with caramel and garnish with crushed salty pretzels.

24 cupcakes

PART 2

Crowd Favorites

What if, as you are embarking on your baking adventures, you encounter a tough crowd? The next recipes will please even the pickiest eater.

Peanut Butter Apple Cupcakes

Fresh apple slices with creamy peanut butter is the easiest snack you can prepare when hunger attacks. If you combine these two ingredients into a cupcake, you have a winner.

My favorite apples for baking are Granny Smith; they are sour and crispy and add great texture to the cupcakes.

Cupcakes

1 cup peeled, cored, diced fresh apple
  (about 1 apple)
3 cups all-purpose flour
1 tablespoon baking powder
½ teaspoon salt
½ cup buttermilk
¼ cup vegetable oil
1 tablespoon vanilla extract
½ teaspoon almond extract
4 ounces unsalted butter (1 stick)
½ cup creamy peanut butter
2 cups sugar
5 large eggs

Peanut Butter Icing

12 ounces unsalted butter
½ cup creamy peanut butter
1 tablespoon vanilla extract
1 teaspoon almond extract
1 lb powdered sugar

Cupcakes

Peel and core the apple and dice into small pieces by hand, or place in the food processor and pulse until you get small pieces. Set aside.

Preheat oven to 325° F. Line a cupcake pan with 24 cupcake liners. Sift flour, baking powder and salt into a bowl and aside. Combine apple, buttermilk, oil, and vanilla and almond extracts in another bowl and set aside.

In the bowl of an electric mixer fitted with the paddle attachment, cream butter, peanut butter and sugar until the mixture is fluffy, about 7 minutes on medium-high speed. Lower the speed to medium and add the eggs, one egg at a time, scraping down the sides of the bowl after each addition until fully incorporated, about 2 minutes. Turn the mixer to a lower speed, then add the flour mixture and the liquids, alternating between the two, beginning and ending with the flour.

Fill the 24 cupcake liners two-thirds full with batter and bake for 20 to 22 minutes, until the cupcakes are golden and baked through. Cool cupcakes completely.

Icing

Whip the butter in the bowl of an electric mixer fitted with the paddle attachment at medium-high speed until the butter is light and fluffy, about 7 minutes. Lower the speed and add the peanut butter, and vanilla and almond extracts and beat until fully incorporated. Stop the mixer and scrape the sides, then add the powdered sugar and beat for 3 more minutes. Stop the mixer and scrape the sides, then mix for 5 more minutes at medium-high speed. Put the icing into a pastry bag fitted with a large metal tip.

To assemble: Allow the cupcakes to fully cool. Pipe on the peanut butter icing.

24 cupcakes

Pumpkin Spice Latte Cupcakes

September comes around and, sooner than you are ready for it, "pumpkin fever" starts; restaurants, bakeries and coffee shops scramble to create succulent soups, pies, and cheesecakes. Everything pumpkin! At that time of year, being the proud coffee lover (addict) I am, I look forward to one thing the most: pumpkin latte. If you have never had one, I highly recommend it. For me, fall doesn't officially start until I have this spicy, creamy and aromatic piece of liquid heaven. This is my cupcake interpretation of the pumpkin latte.

Cupcakes

3 cups all-purpose flour
1 tablespoon baking powder
½ teaspoon salt
3 tablespoons instant coffee granules
½ teaspoon ground cinnamon
½ teaspoon ground nutmeg
½ teaspoon ground ginger
½ cup buttermilk
¾ cup pure canned pumpkin
¼ cup vegetable oil
1 tablespoon vanilla extract
½ teaspoon almond extract
8 ounces unsalted butter (2 sticks)
2 cups sugar
5 large eggs

Coffee Icing

1 lb unsalted butter
2 tablespoons heavy whipping cream
3 tablespoons instant coffee granules
1 tablespoon vanilla extract
1 teaspoon almond extract
¼ teaspoon salt
1 lb powdered sugar

Cupcakes

Preheat oven to 325° F. Line a cupcake pan with 24 cupcake liners. Sift the flour, baking powder, salt, coffee, cinnamon, nutmeg, and ginger into a bowl and set aside. Combine buttermilk, pumpkin, oil, and vanilla and almond extracts in another bowl and set aside.

In the bowl of an electric mixer fitted with the paddle attachment, cream the butter and sugar until the mixture is lighter in color and fluffy, about 7 minutes on medium-high speed. Lower the speed to medium and add the eggs, one egg at a time, scraping down the sides of the bowl after each addition until fully incorporated, about 2 minutes. Turn the mixer to a lower speed, then add the flour mixture and the liquids, alternating between the two, beginning and ending with the flour.

Fill the 24 cupcake liners two-thirds full with batter and bake for 20 to 22 minutes, until the cupcakes are golden and baked through. Cool cupcakes completely.

Icing

Whip the butter in the bowl of an electric mixer fitted with the paddle attachment at medium-high speed until the butter is light and fluffy, about 7 minutes; lower the speed and add the heavy whipping cream, instant coffee, vanilla, almond extract and salt and beat until fully incorporated. Stop the mixer and scrape the sides, then add the powdered sugar and beat for 3 more minutes. Stop the mixer and scrape the sides, then mix for 5 more minutes at medium-high speed. Put the icing into a pastry bag fitted with a large metal tip.

To assemble: Allow the cupcakes to fully cool. Pipe on the coffee icing.

24 cupcakes

French Toast Cupcakes

There is nothing better than waking up to the smell of delicious french toast on a Sunday morning. This cupcake tastes just like it, and the maple buttercream icing is the perfect complement.

Cupcakes

3 cups all-purpose flour
1 tablespoon baking powder
½ teaspoon salt
1 tablespoon ground cinnamon
½ teaspoon ground nutmeg
1 cup buttermilk
¼ cup vegetable oil
1 tablespoon vanilla extract
½ teaspoon almond extract
8 ounces unsalted butter (2 sticks)
2 cups sugar
5 large eggs

Maple Buttercream Icing

1 lb unsalted butter
⅓ cup maple syrup
1 tablespoon vanilla extract
1 teaspoon almond extract
¼ teaspoon salt
1 lb powdered sugar

Cupcakes

Preheat oven to 325° F. Line a cupcake pan with 24 cupcake liners. Sift the flour, baking powder, salt, cinnamon, and nutmeg into a bowl and set aside. Combine buttermilk, oil, and vanilla and almond extracts in another bowl and set aside.

In the bowl of an electric mixer fitted with the paddle attachment, cream the butter and sugar until the mixture is lighter in color and fluffy, about 7 minutes on medium-high speed. Lower the speed to medium and add the eggs, one egg at a time, scraping down the sides of the bowl after each addition until _fully_ incorporated, about 2 minutes. Turn the mixer to a lower speed, then add the flour mixture and the liquids, alternating between the two, beginning and ending with the flour.

Fill the 24 cupcake liners two-thirds full with batter and bake for 20 to 22 minutes, until the cupcakes are golden and baked through. Cool cupcakes completely.

Icing

Whip the butter in the bowl of an electric mixer fitted with the paddle attachment at medium-high speed until the butter is light and fluffy, about 7 minutes; lower the speed and add the maple syrup, vanilla, almond extract and salt and beat until fully incorporated. Stop the mixer and scrape the sides, then add the powdered sugar and beat for 3 more minutes. Stop the mixer and scrape the sides, then mix for 5 more minutes at medium-high speed. Put the icing into a pastry bag fitted with a large metal tip.

To assemble: Allow the cupcakes to fully cool. Pipe on the maple buttercream icing.

24 cupcakes

Banana Chocolate Cupcakes

This cupcake is inspired by frozen chocolate bananas. The caramelized banana icing is absolutely delectable.

Cupcakes

1¾ cup all-purpose flour
¾ cup unsweetened cocoa powder
1½ teaspoon baking powder
1½ teaspoon baking soda
½ teaspoon salt
½ cup buttermilk
½ cup vegetable oil
1 tablespoon vanilla extract
1 teaspoon almond extract
1½ cup mashed bananas
   (the riper the bananas, the better)
2 cups sugar
2 large eggs

Caramelized Banana Filling

2 tablespoons unsalted butter
½ cup brown sugar
3 cups mashed bananas
½ cup water
½ teaspoon ground cinnamon
½ teaspoon ground cloves
¼ teaspoon salt

Caramelized Banana Icing

1 lb unsalted butter
⅓ cup Caramelized Banana Filling
   (recipe above)
1 tablespoon vanilla extract
1 tablespoon banana extract
1 teaspoon almond extract
1 lb powdered sugar

Cupcakes

Preheat oven to 325° F and line a cupcake pan with 24 cupcake liners. Sift the flour, cocoa powder, baking powder, baking soda and salt into a bowl and set aside. Combine buttermilk, oil, and vanilla and almond extracts in another bowl and set aside.

In the bowl of an electric mixer fitted with the paddle attachment, beat the bananas, eggs, and sugar until the eggs are fully incorporated, about 3 minutes on medium speed. Turn the mixer to a lower speed, then add the flour mixture and the liquids, alternating between the two, beginning and ending with the flour.

Fill the 24 cupcake liners two-thirds full with batter and bake for 20 to 22 minutes, until the cupcakes are baked through. Cool cupcakes completely.

Filling

Combine unsalted butter and brown sugar in a small heavy-bottomed saucepan and cook at medium heat until butter and sugar melt. Add mashed bananas, water, ground cinnamon, ground cloves and salt and stir constantly, cooking for 8 to 10 minutes at medium heat until the mixture thickens. Remove the filling from the heat and cool to room temperature. Store in the refrigerator until needed.

Reserve ⅓ cup of the filling to make the icing.

Icing

Whip the butter in the bowl of an electric mixer fitted with the paddle attachment at medium-high speed until the butter is light and fluffy, about 7 minutes. Lower the speed and add the ⅓ cup banana filling, vanilla, banana and almond extracts, and salt and beat until fully incorporated. Stop the mixer and scrape the sides, then add the powdered sugar and beat for 3 more minutes. Stop the mixer and scrape the sides, then mix for 5 more minutes at medium-high speed. Put the icing into a pastry bag fitted with a large metal tip.

Allow the cupcakes to fully cool. Using an apple corer, remove a piece of each cupcake from the center, fill the cupcakes with the caramelized banana filling, and pipe on the banana icing.

24 cupcakes

Caramel Apple Cupcakes

Caramel apple cupcakes are one of our most popular during the fall season. These are the perfect swap for the traditional apple pie.

Cupcakes

3 cups all-purpose flour
1 tablespoon baking powder
½ teaspoon salt
1 tablespoon ground cinnamon
½ teaspoon ground nutmeg
½ cup buttermilk
1 cup peeled, cored, diced fresh apple
    (about 1 Granny Smith apple)
¼ cup vegetable oil
1 tablespoon vanilla extract
½ teaspoon almond extract
8 ounces unsalted butter (2 sticks)
2 cups sugar
5 large eggs

Salted Caramel Filling

See page 31 for recipe and instructions.

Caramel Icing

1 lb unsalted butter
⅓ cup Salted Caramel Filling *(See above)*
1 tablespoon vanilla extract
1 teaspoon almond extract
¼ teaspoon salt
1 lb powdered sugar

Cupcakes

Preheat oven to 325° F and line a cupcake pan with 24 cupcake liners. Sift the flour, baking powder, cinnamon, nutmeg and salt into a bowl and set aside. Combine diced apple, buttermilk, oil, and vanilla and almond extracts in another bowl and set aside.

In the bowl of an electric mixer fitted with the paddle attachment, cream the butter and sugar until the mixture is lighter in color and fluffy, about 7 minutes on medium-high speed. Lower the speed to medium and add the eggs, one egg at a time, scraping down the sides of the bowl after each addition until fully incorporated, about 2 minutes. Turn the mixer to a lower speed, then add the flour mixture and the liquids, alternating between the two, beginning and ending with the flour.

Fill the 24 cupcake liners two-thirds full with batter and bake for 20 to 22 minutes, until the cupcakes are golden and baked through. Cool cupcakes completely.

Icing

Whip the butter in the bowl of an electric mixer fitted with the paddle attachment at medium-high speed until the butter is light and fluffy, about 7 minutes. Lower the speed and add the recipe's yield of Salted Caramel Filling, vanilla and almond extracts, and salt and beat until fully incorporated. Stop the mixer and scrape the sides, then add the powdered sugar and beat for 3 more minutes. Stop the mixer and scrape the sides, then mix for 5 more minutes at medium-high speed. Put the icing into a pastry bag fitted with a large metal tip.

Allow the cupcakes to fully cool. Using an apple corer, remove a piece of each cupcake from the center, fill the cupcakes with the salted caramel filling, and pipe on the caramel icing.

24 cupcakes

Blueberry Pancake Cupcakes

When summer comes along, so do blueberries. Add blueberries to a delicious spiced cupcake and the results are phenomenal!

Cupcakes

3 cups all-purpose flour
1 tablespoon baking powder
½ teaspoon salt
1 tablespoon ground cinnamon
½ teaspoon ground nutmeg
1 cup buttermilk
¼ cup vegetable oil
1 tablespoon vanilla extract
½ teaspoon almond extract
8 ounces unsalted butter (2 sticks)
2 cups sugar
5 large eggs
1 cup fresh blueberries

Blueberry Filling

2 cups fresh blueberries
¼ cup water
½ cup heavy whipping cream
½ cup sugar
2 tablespoons fresh lemon juice
2 tablespoons cornstarch

Cinnamon Sugar

4 tablespoons sugar
2 tablespoons ground cinnamon

Cinnamon Icing

1 lb unsalted butter
2 tablespoons heavy whipping cream
2 tablespoons ground cinnamon
1 tablespoon vanilla extract
1 teaspoon almond extract
¼ teaspoon salt
1 lb powdered sugar

Cupcakes

Preheat oven to 325° F and line a cupcake pan with 24 cupcake liners. Sift the flour, baking powder, salt, cinnamon and, nutmeg into a bowl and set aside. Combine buttermilk, oil, and vanilla and almond extracts in another bowl and set aside.

In the bowl of an electric mixer fitted with the paddle attachment, cream the butter and sugar until the mixture is lighter in color and fluffy, about 7 minutes on medium-high speed. Lower the speed to medium and add the eggs, one egg at a time, scraping down the sides of the bowl after each addition until fully incorporated, about 2 minutes. Turn the mixer to a lower speed, then add the flour mixture and the liquids, alternating between the two, beginning and ending with the flour. Fold in blueberries by hand.

Fill the 24 cupcake liners two-thirds full with batter and bake for 20 to 22 minutes, until the cupcakes are golden and baked through. Cool cupcakes completely.

Filling

Puree blueberries in a food processor and transfer to a heavy-bottomed saucepan. Add water, cream, sugar, and lemon juice and cook at medium heat for 10 to 12 minutes, stirring frequently to keep the blueberries from sticking to the bottom of the pan.

In a separate container dissolve cornstarch in 3 tablespoons of water and whisk together with a fork until all lumps have disappeared. Pour cornstarch mixture into the blueberry mixture, then stir and cook for an additional minute; the filling will thicken immediately.

Remove the filling from the heat and cool to room temperature. Store in the refrigerator until needed.

Cinnamon Sugar

Mix cinnamon and sugar in a container with a lid and shake well until blended.

Icing

Whip the butter in the bowl of an electric mixer fitted with the paddle attachment at medium-high speed until the butter is light and fluffy, about 7 minutes; lower the speed and add the cream, cinnamon, vanilla and almond extracts, and salt and beat until fully incorporated. Stop the mixer and scrape the sides, then add the powdered sugar and beat for 3 more minutes. Stop the mixer and scrape the sides, then mix for 5 more minutes at medium-high speed. Put the icing into a pastry bag fitted with a large metal tip.

Allow the cupcakes to fully cool. Using an apple corer, remove a piece of each cupcake from the center, fill the cupcakes with the blueberry filling, and pipe on the cinnamon icing. Sprinkle with the cinnamon sugar.

24 cupcakes

Fruit Cereal Cupcakes

These cupcakes are kids' number one favorite! They are fun and colorful; the berry and fruity flavors are the perfect combo and the marshmallow icing knocks it out of the park!

Cupcakes

3 cups all-purpose flour
1 tablespoon baking powder
½ teaspoon salt
½ cup strawberry juice
  (or any fruit cocktail juice)
½ cup orange juice
¼ cup vegetable oil
1 tablespoon raspberry extract
1 tablespoon vanilla extract
½ teaspoon almond extract
8 ounces unsalted butter (2 sticks)
2 cups sugar
5 large eggs
2 cups fruit-flavored crisp rice type cereal

Marshmallow Icing

1 lb unsalted butter
1 cup marshmallow creme
1 tablespoon vanilla extract
½ teaspoon almond extract
¼ teaspoon salt
¼ teaspoon red food color (optional)
1 lb powdered sugar

Cupcakes

Preheat oven to 325° F and line a cupcake pan with 24 cupcake liners. Sift the flour, baking powder and salt into a bowl and set aside. Combine strawberry or fruit cocktail juice with orange juice, oil, raspberry, and vanilla and almond extracts in another bowl and set aside.

In the bowl of an electric mixer fitted with the paddle attachment, cream the butter and sugar until the mixture is lighter in color and fluffy, about 7 minutes on medium-high speed. Lower the speed to medium and add the eggs, one egg at a time, scraping down the sides of the bowl after each addition until fully incorporated, about 2 minutes. Turn the mixer to a lower speed, then add the flour mixture and the liquids, alternating between the two, beginning and ending with the flour. Fold the cereal into the batter by hand.

Fill the 24 cupcake liners two-thirds full with batter and bake for 20 to 22 minutes, until the cupcakes are golden and baked through. Cool cupcakes completely.

Icing

Whip the butter in the bowl of an electric mixer fitted with the paddle attachment at medium-high speed until the butter is light and fluffy, about 7 minutes. Lower the speed and add the marshmallow creme, vanilla and almond extracts, salt, and red food color (if using) and beat until fully incorporated. Stop the mixer and scrape the sides, then add the powdered sugar and beat for 3 more minutes. Stop the mixer and scrape the sides, then mix for 5 more minutes at medium-high speed. Put the icing into a pastry bag fitted with a large metal tip.

To assemble: Allow the cupcakes to fully cool. Pipe on the marshmallow icing.

24 cupcakes

PART 3

Vegetable / Savory

Most likely, cupcakes are not the first thing that comes to mind when you see vegetables, right? But vegetables can be used in both sweet and savory baking with great success! Give it a try and you'll be pleasantly surprised.

The main difference between muffins (where you may a be a little more familiar with using vegetables, like corn or zucchini) and cupcakes is the texture. Muffins are dense, and cupcakes are light and fluffy due to the creaming of the butter and sugar at the beginning of the process.

Spinach Cupcakes

These spinach cupcakes have the perfect amount of sweetness, a naturally bright green color, and a subtle yet tasty spinach flavor. The strawberry icing adds a great visual contrast and fresh fruity flavor.

Cupcakes

3 cups all-purpose flour
1 tablespoon baking powder
½ teaspoon salt
1½ cup fresh spinach, finely chopped
¾ cup buttermilk
¼ cup vegetable oil
1 tablespoon vanilla extract
½ teaspoon almond extract
8 ounces unsalted butter (2 sticks)
2 cups sugar
5 large eggs

Blueberry Filling

See page 51 for recipe and instructions.

Strawberry Icing

1 lb unsalted butter
4 medium strawberries, chopped into
    small pieces
1 tablespoon vanilla extract
1 tablespoon strawberry extract
½ teaspoon almond extract
¼ teaspoon salt
1 lb powdered sugar
5 drops red food coloring (optional)

Cupcakes

Preheat oven to 325° F and line a cupcake pan with 24 cupcake liners. Sift the flour, baking powder, and salt into a bowl; add chopped spinach and set aside.

Combine buttermilk, oil, and vanilla and almond extracts in another bowl and set aside. In the bowl of an electric mixer fitted with the paddle attachment, cream the butter and sugar until the mixture is lighter in color and fluffy, about 7 minutes on medium-high speed. Lower the speed to medium and add the eggs, one egg at a time, scraping down the sides of the bowl after each addition until fully incorporated, about 2 minutes. Turn the mixer to a lower speed, then add the flour mixture and the liquids, alternating between the two, beginning and ending with the flour.

Fill the 24 cupcake liners two-thirds full with batter and bake for 20 to 22 minutes, until the cupcakes are golden and baked through. Cool cupcakes completely.

Icing

Whip the butter in the bowl of an electric mixer fitted with the paddle attachment at medium-high speed until the butter is light and fluffy, about 7 minutes; lower the speed and add the chopped strawberries, vanilla, strawberry and almond extracts, salt, and food coloring (if using) and beat until fully incorporated; stop the mixer and scrape the sides, add the powdered sugar and beat for 3 more minutes. Stop and scrape the sides of the mixer and mix for 5 more minutes at medium-high speed. Put the icing into a pastry bag fitted with a large metal tip.

To assemble: Allow the cupcakes to fully cool. Using an apple corer, remove a piece of each cupcake from the center, fill the cupcakes with blueberry filling, and pipe on the strawberry icing.

24 cupcakes

Ham and Pineapple Cupcakes

I must admit, I was not originally a believer in savory cupcakes. I thought "What's the point?" But when I decided to give it a try, my first instinct was to add an element of sweetness to complement the salty and savory flavors. I turned to my favorite sweet-savory food for inspiration: the Hawaiian pizza! Chunky pieces of sweet pineapple and salty ham...how can you say no?!

Cupcakes

3 cups all-purpose flour
1 tablespoon baking powder
½ teaspoon salt
½ cup (4 ounces) smoked ham,
finely chopped
1 can (20 ounces) pineapple chunks,
  drained
½ cup shredded mozzarella cheese
4 ounces unsalted butter (1 stick)
5 large eggs

Cupcakes

Preheat oven to 325° F and line a cupcake pan with 24 cupcake liners. Sift the flour, baking powder, and salt into a bowl and set aside. Chop pineapple chunks into small pieces and combine with ham and mozzarella cheese in another bowl and set aside.

In the bowl of an electric mixer fitted with the paddle attachment, cream the butter until light and fluffy, about 7 minutes on medium-high speed. Lower the speed to medium and add the eggs, one egg at a time, scraping down the sides of the bowl after each addition until fully incorporated, about 2 minutes. Turn the mixer to a lower speed, then add the flour mixture and the pineapple mixture, alternating between the two, beginning and ending with the flour.

Fill the 24 cupcake liners two-thirds full with batter and bake for 22 to 25 minutes, until the cupcakes are golden and baked through. Serve warm.

24 cupcakes

Corn and Jalapeño Cupcakes

If you drive through Pennsylvania you will see never ending corn fields everywhere. The state is such a great producer of corn and I couldn't be happier. Corn is one of my favorite foods ever. I love not only the taste but the smell of corn, and I try to incorporate it in most of my cooking; salads, soups, meat, and now cupcakes! This cupcake is inspired by a delicious savory corn fritter.

2½ cups all-purpose flour
½ cup corn meal
1 tablespoon baking powder
½ teaspoon salt
1½ teaspoons cumin seeds
1 cup canned sweet corn, drained
1 jalapeño pepper, minced
1 cup sour cream
½ cup vegetable oil
5 large eggs

Preheat oven to 325° F and line a cupcake pan with 24 cupcake liners. Sift the flour, corn meal, baking powder, and salt into a bowl, add cumin and set aside. Combine corn, jalapeño pepper, sour cream and oil in another bowl and set aside.

In the bowl of an electric mixer fitted with the paddle attachment, beat eggs at medium speed until fully mixed, about 2 minutes. Turn the mixer to a lower speed, then add the flour mixture and the corn mixture, alternating between the two, beginning and ending with the flour.

Fill the 24 cupcake liners two-thirds full with batter and bake for 20 to 22 minutes, until the cupcakes are golden and baked through. Serve warm.

24 cupcakes

Tomatoes and Basil Cupcakes

This tomato cupcake is inspired by a freshly baked Margherita pizza; sweet tomatoes, fresh basil and mozzarella...Mangia!

Cupcakes

3 cups all-purpose flour
1 tablespoon baking powder
½ teaspoon salt
½ teaspoon black pepper
1 cup cherry tomatoes, halved
½ cup fresh basil, chopped
⅓ cup shredded Parmesan cheese
½ cup mozzarella cheese, cubed
½ cup buttermilk
¼ cup vegetable oil
8 ounces unsalted butter (2 sticks)
5 large eggs

Cupcakes

Preheat oven to 325° F and line a cupcake pan with 24 cupcake liners. Sift the flour, baking powder, salt and black pepper into a bowl and set aside.

Combine tomatoes, basil, Parmesan cheese, mozzarella cheese, buttermilk, and oil in another bowl and set aside.

In the bowl of an electric mixer fitted with the paddle attachment, cream the butter until light and fluffy, about 7 minutes on medium-high speed. Lower the speed to medium and add the eggs, one egg at a time, scraping down the sides of the bowl after each addition until fully incorporated, about 2 minutes. Turn the mixer to a lower speed, then add the flour mixture and the liquids, alternating between the two, beginning and ending with the flour.

Fill the 24 cupcake liners two-thirds full with batter and bake for 20 to 22 minutes, until the cupcakes are golden and baked through. Serve warm.

24 cupcakes

Three Peppers Cupcakes

Colorful and cheesy, this cupcake is a fantastic substitution of the typical dinner roll and the Parmesan cheese on top adds a great salty crust.

Cupcakes

3 cups all-purpose flour
1 tablespoon baking powder
½ teaspoon salt
½ teaspoon black ground pepper
½ cup diced orange pepper
½ cup diced yellow pepper
½ cup diced red pepper
½ cup mozzarella cheese, cubed
½ cup Parmesan cheese, shredded
½ cup buttermilk
¼ cup vegetable oil
8 ounces unsalted butter (2 sticks)
5 large eggs

Cupcakes

Preheat oven to 325° F and line a cupcake pan with 24 cupcake liners. Sift the flour, baking powder, salt and black pepper into a bowl, and set aside. Combine orange, yellow and red pepper, mozzarella cheese, buttermilk, and oil in another bowl and set aside.

In the bowl of an electric mixer fitted with the paddle attachment, cream the butter until light and fluffy, about 7 minutes on medium-high speed. Lower the speed to medium and add the eggs, one egg at a time, scraping down the sides of the bowl after each addition until fully incorporated, about 2 minutes. Turn the mixer to a lower speed, then add the flour mixture and the liquids, alternating between the two, beginning and ending with the flour.

Fill the 24 cupcake liners two-thirds full with batter and sprinkle with Parmesan cheese. Bake for 20 to 22 minutes, until the cupcakes are golden and baked through. Serve warm.

24 cupcakes

Salmon Cupcakes

Yes, you read it correctly: Salmon! Bagel and smoked salmon is one of my favorite brunch menu items. This is my cupcake interpretation; the salmon is the star and the cream and capers icing adds the perfect amount of acidity. Pair these cupcakes with a mimosa on a fabulous lazy Sunday.

Cupcakes

3 cups all-purpose flour
1 tablespoon baking powder
6 ounces smoked salmon, chopped
½ cup sour cream
1 cup vegetable oil
5 large eggs

Cream Cheese and Capers Icing

12 ounces cream cheese
2 tablespoons capers, chopped
2 tablespoons fresh lemon juice
black pepper to taste

Cupcakes

Preheat oven to 325° F and line a cupcake pan with 24 cupcake liners. Sift the flour, baking powder into a bowl, and set aside. Combine salmon, sour cream, and oil in another bowl and set aside.

In the bowl of an electric mixer fitted with the paddle attachment, beat eggs until combined, about 2 minutes at medium speed. Turn the mixer to a lower speed, then add the flour mixture and the liquids, alternating between the two, beginning and ending with the flour. Fill the 24 cupcake liners two-thirds full with batter. Bake for 20 to 22 minutes, until the cupcakes are golden and baked through.

Icing

Whip the cream cheese in the bowl of an electric mixer fitted with the paddle attachment until fluffy, about 5 minutes on medium-high speed; turn mixer to low speed and add capers, lemon juice and pepper, beat until fully incorporated. Put the icing into a pastry bag with a large metal tip. Pipe a small dollop of icing on each cupcake.

24 cupcakes

Carrot & Beets Cupcakes

This cupcake is inspired by the juice my mom used to make when I was growing up. It's made with carrots, red beets, and oranges, so it is supposed to help with vitality and energy. And it's a great way to incorporate vegetables into a tasty cupcake.

68

Cupcakes

3 cups all-purpose flour
1 tablespoon baking powder
½ teaspoon salt
2 cups shredded carrots
1 cup pureed canned red beets
½ cup orange juice
¼ cup vegetable oil
1 tablespoon vanilla extract
1 teaspoon almond extract
8 ounces unsalted butter (2 sticks)
2 cups sugar
5 large eggs

Beet Icing

1 lb unsalted butter
⅓ cup beet puree
1 tablespoons orange extract
1 tablespoon vanilla extract
¼ teaspoon salt
1 lb powdered sugar

Cupcakes

Preheat oven to 325° F. Line a cupcake pan with 24 cupcake liners. Sift the flour, baking powder and salt into a bowl, add the shredded carrots, and set aside.

Combine the beet puree, orange juice, oil, and vanilla and almond extracts in another bowl and set aside.

In the bowl of an electric mixer fitted with the paddle attachment, cream the butter and sugar until the mixture is lighter in color and fluffy, about 7 minutes on medium-high speed. Lower the speed to medium and add the eggs, one egg at a time, scraping down the sides of the bowl after each addition until fully incorporated, about 2 minutes. Turn the mixer to a lower speed, then add the flour mixture and the beets mixture, alternating between the two, beginning and ending with the flour.

Fill the 24 cupcake liners two-thirds full with batter and bake for 20 to 22 minutes, until the cupcakes are baked through. Cool cupcakes completely.

Icing

Whip the butter in the bowl of an electric mixer fitted with the paddle attachment at medium-high speed until it is light and fluffy, about 7 minutes. Lower the speed and add the beet puree, orange and vanilla extracts, and salt and beat until fully incorporated. Stop the mixer and scrape the sides, then add the powdered sugar and beat for 3 more minutes. Stop the mixer and scrape the sides, then mix for 5 more minutes at medium-high speed. Put the icing into a pastry bag fitted with a large metal tip.

To assemble: Allow the cupcakes to fully cool, and pipe on the beet icing.

24 cupcakes

PART 4

Cocktail Inspired

Cocktails offer a well of baking inspiration, and they can be easily interpreted into a cupcake; the festive combination of liquor and common ingredient such as fruits, nuts or chocolate makes it easy to prepare.

Peach Bellini Cupcake

If you have never had a peach bellini you should definitely start sipping on one, and while you are at it you can start whipping up this lovely cupcake creation. It's light, summery, fruity and absolutely delightful. The perfect cupcake for a bridal shower or a girls' night in.

Cupcakes

3 cups all-purpose flour
1 tablespoon baking powder
½ teaspoon salt
¼ cup peach schnapps
½ cup Champagne (or dry sparkling wine)
¼ cup vegetable oil
1 tablespoon vanilla extract
8 ounces unsalted butter (2 sticks)
2 cups sugar
5 large eggs

Peach Filling

2 medium size peaches
½ cup peach schnapps
½ cup Champagne (or dry sparkling wine)
½ cup sugar
1 tablespoon vanilla extract
2 tablespoons cornstarch

Peach Icing

1 lb unsalted butter
½ cup peach filling
1 tablespoon vanilla extract
1 teaspoon almond extract
¼ teaspoon salt
1 lb powdered sugar

Cupcakes

Preheat oven to 325° F and line a cupcake pan with 24 cupcake liners. Sift the flour, baking powder, and salt into a bowl and set aside. Combine Peach Schnapps, Champagne, oil, and vanilla extract in another bowl and set aside.

In the bowl of an electric mixer fitted with the paddle attachment, cream the butter and sugar until the mixture is lighter in color and fluffy, about 7 minutes on medium-high speed. Lower the speed to medium and add the eggs, one egg at a time, scraping down the sides of the bowl after each addition until fully incorporated, about 2 minutes. Turn the mixer to a lower speed, then add the flour mixture and the liquids, alternating between the two, beginning and ending with the flour.

Fill the 24 cupcake liners two-thirds full with batter and bake for 20 to 22 minutes, until the cupcakes are golden and baked through. Cool cupcakes completely.

Filling

Peel the peaches and cut in cubes, removing and discarding the pits. Place peaches in a food processor and blend until you get a soft puree. Place peach puree in a heavy-bottomed saucepan and add peach schnapps, Champagne, sugar, and vanilla extract, stirring frequently to keep the peaches from sticking to the bottom of the pan. Cook for approximately 10 to 12 minutes at medium temperature. Dissolve cornstarch in 2 tablespoons of water and whisk together until all lumps have disappeared, then pour into the peaches mixture, and stir and cook for an additional minute until mixture thickens. Remove the filling from the heat and cool to room temperature. Reserve ½ cup of the filling for the icing. Store in the refrigerator until needed.

Icing

Whip the butter in the bowl of an electric mixer fitted with the paddle attachment at medium-high speed until the butter is light and fluffy, about 7 minutes; lower the speed and add the peach filling, vanilla and almond extracts, and salt and beat until fully incorporated. Stop the mixer and scrape the sides. Add the powdered sugar and beat for 3 more minutes. Stop the mixer and scrape the sides, then mix for 5 more minutes at medium-high speed. Put the icing into a pastry bag fitted with a large metal tip.

Allow the cupcakes to fully cool. Using an apple corer, remove a piece of each cupcake from the center, fill the cupcakes with the peach filling and pipe the peach icing.

24 cupcakes

Strawberry Colada Cupcakes

This cupcake is inspired by a piña colada, but it features sweet strawberries and of course coconut! Daydreaming of laying on the beach drinking strawberry colada? Whip up this summery treat, muy delicioso!

74

Cupcakes

3 cups all-purpose flour
1 tablespoon baking powder
½ teaspoon salt
½ cup unsweetened shredded coconut
¾ cup fresh strawberries puree,
    about 4 to 5 strawberries
½ cup dark rum
¼ cup vegetable oil
1 tablespoon strawberry extract
1 tablespoon vanilla extract
½ teaspoon almond extract
8 ounces unsalted butter (2 sticks)
2 cups sugar
5 large eggs
Maraschino cherries with stems
    for garnish

Coconut Cream Cheese Icing

8 ounces unsalted butter (2 sticks)
8 ounces cream cheese
2 tablespoons coconut extract
1 tablespoon vanilla extract
½ teaspoon almond extract
¼ teaspoon salt
1 lb powdered sugar

Pink Coconut Garnish

2 cups unsweetened shredded coconut
Liquid red food coloring

Cupcakes

Preheat oven to 325° F and line a cupcake pan with 24 cupcake liners. Sift the flour, baking powder, and salt into a bowl, add shredded coconut and set aside. Puree strawberries in a food processor and combine with rum, oil, and vanilla, strawberry and almond extracts in another bowl and set aside.

In the bowl of an electric mixer fitted with the paddle attachment, cream the butter and sugar until the mixture is lighter in color and fluffy, about 7 minutes on medium-high speed. Lower the speed to medium and add the eggs, one egg at a time, scraping down the sides of the bowl after each addition until fully incorporated, about 2 minutes. Turn the mixer to a lower speed, then add the flour mixture and the liquids, alternating between the two, beginning and ending with the flour.

Fill the 24 cupcake liners two-thirds full with batter and bake for 20 to 22 minutes, until the cupcakes are golden and baked through. Cool cupcakes completely.

Icing

Whip the butter in the bowl of an electric mixer fitted with the paddle attachment at medium-high speed until the butter is light and fluffy, about 7 minutes; lower the speed and add the cream cheese, coconut, vanilla and almond extracts, and salt and beat until fully incorporated; stop the mixer and scrape the sides, add the powdered sugar and beat for 3 more minutes. Stop and scrape the sides of the mixer and mix for 5 more minutes at medium-high speed. Put the icing into a pastry bag fitted with a large metal tip.

Pink Coconut Garnish

Place shredded coconut in a container with a lid, dissolve 5 drops of food coloring in 3 tablespoons of water and add to coconut, cover the container with the lid and shake well until the coconut turns pink.

To assemble: Allow the cupcakes to fully cool. Pipe on the coconut cream cheese icing, and cover with the pink coconut garnish. Top each cupcake with a maraschino cherry.

24 cupcakes

Mojito Cupcakes

There's no more appropriate cocktail on a hot summer night than a mojito, and this cupcake highlights the lightness and the refreshing qualities of the drink itself.

Cupcakes

3 cups all-purpose flour
1 tablespoon baking powder
½ teaspoon salt
3 tablespoons fresh mint, finely chopped
½ cup buttermilk
¼ cup lime juice
¼ cup dark rum
¼ cup vegetable oil
1 tablespoon vanilla extract
1 teaspoon lime extract
½ teaspoon almond extract
8 ounces unsalted butter (2 sticks)
2 cups sugar
5 large eggs

Mint and Lime Icing

1 lb unsalted butter
3 tablespoons dark rum
1 tablespoon fresh lime juice
1 tablespoon fresh mint finely chopped
1 tablespoon vanilla extract
1 teaspoon lime extract
1½ teaspoons mint extract
¼ teaspoon salt
½ teaspoon green food coloring
  (optional)
1 lb powdered sugar

Lime Sugar Garnish

3 limes
½ cup granulated sugar

Cupcakes

Preheat oven to 325° F and line a cupcake pan with 24 cupcake liners. Sift the flour, baking powder, and salt into a bowl, add the chopped mint and set aside. Combine buttermilk, lime juice, dark rum, oil, and vanilla, lime and almond extracts in another bowl and set aside. In the bowl of an electric mixer fitted with the paddle attachment, cream the butter and sugar until the mixture is lighter in color and fluffy, about 7 minutes on medium-high speed. Lower the speed to medium and add the eggs, one egg at a time, scraping down the sides of the bowl after each addition until fully incorporated, about 2 minutes. Turn the mixer to a lower speed, then add the flour mixture and the liquids, alternating between the two, beginning and ending with the flour.

Fill the 24 cupcake liners two-thirds full with batter and bake for 20 to 22 minutes, until the cupcakes are golden and baked through. Cool cupcakes completely.

Icing

Whip the butter in the bowl of an electric mixer fitted with the paddle attachment at medium-high speed until the butter is light and fluffy, about 7 minutes; lower the speed and add rum, lime juice, mint, vanilla and lime extracts, salt and food coloring (if using) and beat until fully incorporated; stop the mixer and scrape the sides, add the powdered sugar and beat for 3 more minutes. Stop and scrape the sides of the mixer and mix for 5 more minutes at medium-high speed. Put the icing into a pastry bag fitted with a large metal tip.

Garnish

Zest the limes and combine the lime zest with the sugar, place in an airtight container, and shake well.

To assemble: Allow the cupcakes to fully cool. Pipe on the mint and lime icing and sprinkle with lime sugar.

24 cupcakes

Margarita Cupcakes

This refreshing cupcake is a
fabulous mix of golden tequila and
lime. The perfect cupcake for your
Cinco de Mayo fiesta—or any time!

Cupcakes

3 cups all-purpose flour
1 tablespoon baking powder
½ teaspoon salt
½ cup buttermilk
¼ cup lime juice
¼ cup tequila
¼ cup vegetable oil
1 tablespoon vanilla extract
1 teaspoon orange extract
½ teaspoon almond extract
8 ounces unsalted butter (2 sticks)
2 cups sugar
5 large eggs

Lime and Tequila Icing

1 lb unsalted butter
3 tablespoons golden tequila
3 tablespoons fresh lime juice
1 tablespoon vanilla extract
1 tablespoon lime extract
1 teaspoon almond extract
¼ teaspoon salt
½ teaspoon green food coloring
   (optional)
1 lb powdered sugar

Lime Sugar Garnish
(See recipe and instructions on page 77)

Cupcakes

Preheat oven to 325° F and line a cupcake pan with 24 cupcake liners. Sift the flour, baking powder, and salt into a bowl and set aside. Combine buttermilk, lime juice, tequila, oil, and vanilla, orange and almond extracts in another bowl and set aside.

In the bowl of an electric mixer fitted with the paddle attachment, cream the butter and sugar until the mixture is lighter in color and fluffy, about 7 minutes on medium-high speed. Lower the speed to medium and add the eggs, one egg at a time, scraping down the sides of the bowl after each addition until fully incorporated, about 2 minutes. Turn the mixer to a lower speed, then add the flour mixture and the liquids, alternating between the two, beginning and ending with the flour.

Fill the 24 cupcake liners two-thirds full with batter and bake for 20 to 22 minutes, until the cupcakes are golden and baked through. Cool cupcakes completely.

Icing

Whip the butter in the bowl of an electric mixer fitted with the paddle attachment at medium-high speed until the butter is light and fluffy, about 7 minutes. Lower the speed and add the tequila, lime juice, vanilla, lime and almond extracts, salt and food coloring (if using) and beat until fully incorporated. Stop the mixer and scrape the sides, then add the powdered sugar and beat for 3 more minutes. Stop the mixer and scrape the sides, then mix for 5 more minutes at medium-high speed. Put the icing into a pastry bag fitted with a large metal tip.

To assemble: Allow the cupcakes to fully cool. Pipe on the lime and tequila icing, and rim each cupcake with lime sugar.

24 cupcakes

Mimosa Cupcakes

Flirty and sparkly, these are a sure hit for your next celebration.

Cupcakes

3 cups all-purpose flour
1 tablespoon baking powder
½ teaspoon salt
2 tablespoons orange puree (*See note*)
¾ cup Champagne
¼ cup vegetable oil
1 tablespoon vanilla extract
1 tablespoon orange extract
8 ounces unsalted butter (2 sticks)
2 cups sugar
5 large eggs

Strawberry Filling

2 cups fresh strawberries, chopped
½ cup water
½ cup granulated sugar
2 tablespoons fresh lemon juice
2 tablespoons cornstarch

Orange Icing

1 lb unsalted butter
¼ cup orange puree (*See note*)
1 tablespoon vanilla extract
1 tablespoon orange extract
1 teaspoon almond extract
½ teaspoon orange food coloring (optional)
¼ teaspoon salt
1 lb powdered sugar

Note: To make orange puree, cut 1 medium seedless orange in half and then cut each half in four pieces. Blend in a food processor with ¼ cup of water until you get a soft puree. You will need 2 tablespoons of puree for the cupcakes and ¼ cup for the icing; you can freeze any leftover puree for future use.

Cupcakes

Preheat oven to 325° F. Line a cupcake pan with 24 cupcake liners. Sift the flour, baking powder and salt into a bowl and set aside. Combine orange puree, Champagne, oil, and vanilla and orange extracts in another bowl and set aside.

In the bowl of an electric mixer fitted with the paddle attachment, cream the butter and sugar until the mixture is lighter in color and fluffy, about 7 minutes on medium-high speed. Lower the speed to medium and add the eggs, one egg at a time, scraping down the sides of the bowl after each addition until fully incorporated, about 2 minutes. Turn the mixer to a lower speed, then add the flour mixture and the liquids, alternating between the two, beginning and ending with the flour.

Fill the 24 cupcake liners two-thirds full with batter and bake for 20 to 22 minutes, until the cupcakes are golden and baked through. Cool cupcakes completely.

Filling

Place chopped strawberries in a heavy-bottomed saucepan and add water, sugar, and lemon juice. Cook on medium heat for approximately 10 to 12 minutes, stirring frequently to keep the strawberries from sticking to the bottom of the pan.

Dissolve cornstarch in 2 tablespoons of water, and whisk together until all lumps have disappeared. Pour into the strawberry mixture, stir and cook for an additional minute until mixture thickens. Remove the filling from the heat and cool to room temperature. Store in the refrigerator until needed.

Icing

Whip the butter in the bowl of an electric mixer fitted with the paddle attachment at medium-high speed until the butter is light and fluffy, about 7 minutes. Lower the speed and add the orange puree, vanilla, orange and almond extracts, salt and food coloring (if using) and beat until fully incorporated. Stop the mixer and scrape the sides, then add the powdered sugar and beat for 3 more minutes. Stop the mixer and scrape the sides, then mix for 5 more minutes at medium-high speed. Put the icing into a pastry bag fitted with a large metal tip.

To assemble: Allow the cupcakes to fully cool. Using an apple corer, remove a piece of each cupcake from the center, fill the cupcakes with the strawberry filling, and pipe on the orange icing.

24 cupcakes

Almond Amaretto Cupcakes

I'm a huge fan of creamy cocktails, and this cocktail-inspired cupcake is spiked with delicious amaretto liqueur. The nutty flavor of the almonds truly enhances the amaretto flavor and adds great texture.

Cupcakes

3 cups all-purpose flour
1 tablespoon baking powder
½ teaspoon salt
½ cup chopped almonds
¾ cup buttermilk
¼ cup amaretto liqueur
¼ cup vegetable oil
1 tablespoon vanilla extract
1 tablespoon almond extract
8 ounces unsalted butter (2 sticks)
2 cups sugar
5 large eggs

Amaretto Icing

1 lb unsalted butter
¼ cup amaretto liqueur
1 tablespoon vanilla extract
1 teaspoon almond extract
¼ teaspoon salt
1 lb powdered sugar

Cupcakes

Preheat oven to 325° F. Line a cupcake pan with 24 cupcake liners. Sift the flour, baking powder and salt into a bowl, add the chopped almonds and set aside.

Combine buttermilk, amaretto, oil, and vanilla and almond extracts in another bowl and set aside.

In the bowl of an electric mixer fitted with the paddle attachment, cream the butter and sugar until the mixture is lighter in color and fluffy, about 7 minutes on medium-high speed. Lower the speed to medium and add the eggs, one egg at a time, scraping down the sides of the bowl after each addition until fully incorporated, about 2 minutes. Turn the mixer to a lower speed, then add the flour mixture and the liquids, alternating between the two, beginning and ending with the flour.

Fill the 24 cupcake liners two-thirds full with batter and bake for 20 to 22 minutes, until the cupcakes are golden and baked through. Cool cupcakes completely.

Icing

Whip the butter in the bowl of an electric mixer fitted with the paddle attachment at medium-high speed until the butter is light and fluffy, about 7 minutes. Lower the speed and add amaretto, vanilla and almond extracts, and salt and beat until fully incorporated. Stop the mixer and scrape the sides, then add the powdered sugar and beat for 3 more minutes. Stop the mixer and scrape the sides, then mix for 5 more minutes at medium-high speed. Put the icing into a pastry bag fitted with a large metal tip.

To assemble: Allow the cupcakes to fully cool, then pipe on the amaretto icing.

24 cupcakes

Chocolate Whiskey Cupcakes

When I asked Sam to tell me what his ideal cupcake would be, he quickly responded "Whiskey!" So I decided to create this cupcake and keep it simple by incorporating the whiskey into a delicious and moist chocolate cake. The cupcake is dipped into a silky whiskey-infused chocolate ganache.

Cupcakes

1¾ cup all-purpose flour
¾ cup unsweetened cocoa powder
1½ teaspoon baking powder
1½ teaspoon baking soda
½ teaspoon salt
1½ cup buttermilk
½ cup whiskey
½ cup vegetable oil
2 cups sugar
1 tablespoon vanilla extract
1 teaspoon almond extract
2 large eggs

Whiskey Ganache

2 cups semisweet chocolate chips
2 cups heavy whipping cream
2 tablespoons unsalted butter
½ cup whiskey

Cupcakes

Preheat oven to 325° F and line a cupcake pan with 24 cupcake liners. Sift the flour, cocoa powder, baking powder, baking soda and salt into a bowl.

Combine buttermilk, whiskey, oil, and vanilla and almond extracts in another bowl and set aside.

In the bowl of an electric mixer fitted with the paddle attachment, mix eggs and sugar until the eggs are fully incorporated, about 3 minutes on medium speed. Turn the mixer to a lower speed, then add the flour mixture and the liquids, alternating between the two, beginning and ending with the flour.

Fill the 24 cupcake liners two-thirds full with batter and bake for 20 to 22 minutes, until the cupcakes are baked through. Cool cupcakes completely.

Ganache

Combine semisweet chocolate chips, cream and butter in a heatproof glass bowl and cook on top of double boiler, stirring constantly until all the chocolate has melted. Stir in whiskey. (You can also combine the chips and cream in a microwave-safe glass bowl and microwave in increments of 30 seconds, stirring in between, until the chocolate is completely melted. Then stir in the butter until completely melted. Stir in whiskey.)

To assemble: Allow the cupcakes to fully cool. Let the ganache cool down until lukewarm. Using an apple corer, remove a piece of each cupcake from the center, fill the cupcakes with the ganache, then dip the top of each cupcake individually into the remaining ganache to cover the top.

24 cupcakes

Limoncello Cupcakes

The aromatic limoncello and basil flavors add a refreshing summertime taste, and the tart raspberry filling makes this combination light and fresh like summer breezes.

Cupcakes

3 cups all-purpose flour
1 tablespoon baking powder
½ teaspoon salt
Zest of one lemon
2 tablespoons chopped fresh basil
½ cup limoncello liqueur
½ cup buttermilk
¼ cup vegetable oil
1 tablespoon vanilla extract
8 ounces unsalted butter (2 sticks)
2 cups sugar
5 large eggs

Raspberry Filling

2 cups raspberries
  (thawed and drained, if using frozen)
½ cup water
½ cup granulated sugar
2 tablespoons cornstarch

Limoncello Icing

1 lb unsalted butter
¼ cup limoncello liqueur
1 tablespoon vanilla extract
¼ teaspoon salt
1 lb powdered sugar

Cupcakes

Preheat oven to 325° F. Line a cupcake pan with 24 cupcake liners. Sift the flour, baking powder and salt into a bowl, add lemon zest and chopped fresh basil and set aside.

Combine limoncello, buttermilk, oil, and vanilla extract in another bowl and set aside. In the bowl of an electric mixer fitted with the paddle attachment, cream the butter and sugar until the mixture is lighter in color and fluffy, about 7 minutes on medium-high speed. Lower the speed to medium and add the eggs, one egg at a time, scraping down the sides of the bowl after each addition until fully incorporated, about 2 minutes. Turn the mixer to a lower speed, then add the flour mixture and then the liquids, alternating between the two, beginning and ending with the flour.

Fill the 24 cupcake liners two-thirds full with batter and bake for 20 to 22 minutes, until the cupcakes are golden and baked through. Cool cupcakes completely.

Filling

Place raspberries in a heavy-bottomed saucepan. Add water and sugar and cook on medium heat for approximately 10 minutes, stirring frequently to keep the raspberries from sticking to the bottom of the pan. Dissolve cornstarch in 2 tablespoons of water, and whisk together until all lumps have disappeared. Pour into the raspberry mixture, stir and cook for an additional minute until mixture thickens.

Remove the filling from the heat and cool to room temperature. Store in the refrigerator until needed.

Icing

Whip the butter in the bowl of an electric mixer fitted with the paddle attachment at medium-high speed until the butter is light and fluffy, about 7 minutes. Lower the speed and add limoncello, vanilla and salt and beat until fully incorporated. Stop the mixer and scrape the sides, then add the powdered sugar and beat for 3 more minutes. Stop the mixer and scrape the sides, then mix for 5 more minutes at medium-high speed. Put the icing into a pastry bag fitted with a large metal tip.

To assemble: Allow the cupcakes to fully cool. Using an apple corer, remove a piece of each cupcake from the center, fill the cupcakes with the raspberry filling, and pipe on the limoncello icing.

24 cupcakes

Index

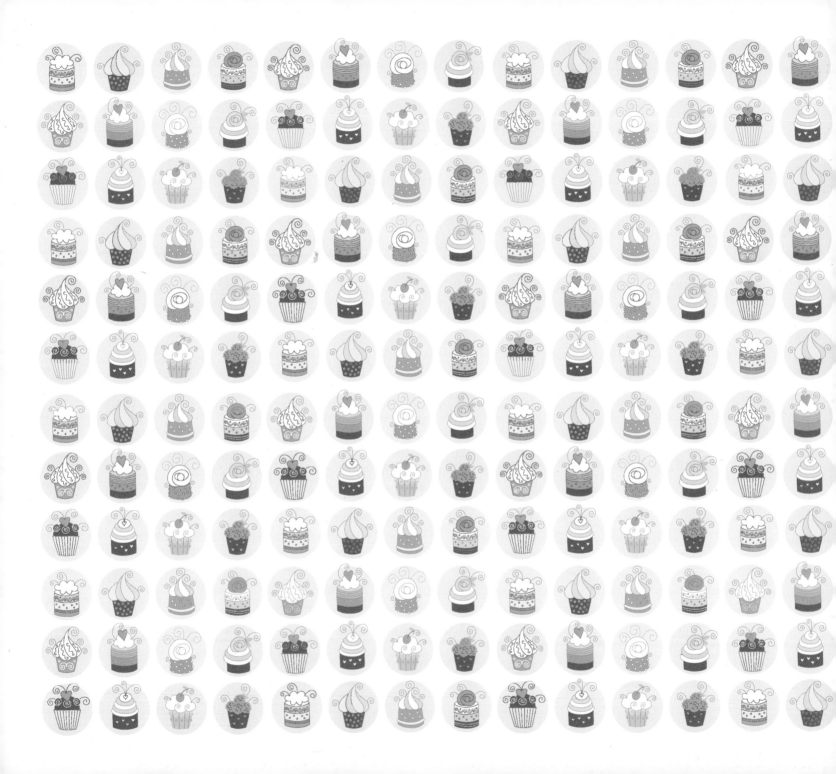